healthy home cooking
for kids

no butter
no white flour
no added sugar

snacks

meals

sides

fruit snacks

birthday party treats

EMILY ROSE BROTT

EBURY
PRESS

An Ebury Press book
Published by Random House Australia Pty Ltd
Level 3, 100 Pacific Highway, North Sydney NSW 2060
www.randomhouse.com.au

First published by Ebury Press in 2013

National Library of Australia
Cataloguing-in-Publication Entry
Brott, Emily Rose, author.
Healthy home cooking for kids/Emily Rose Brott.
ISBN 978 1 74275 999 9 (paperback)
Children – Nutrition.
Cooking.
Cooking (Natural foods)
641.5622

Cover and internal design by Christa Moffitt
Photography and styling by Emily Rose Brott
Printed in China by 1010 Printing International Ltd.

contents

SNACK TIME

MEALS

SIDES

FRUIT SNACKS

BIRTHDAY PARTY TREATS

INTRODUCTION

When it comes to our children, as parents we only want what's best for them. Home cooking allows me to know what is in the food I am serving to my kids, and to make sure that the food I am putting into their bodies is healthy.

I have always cooked healthy meals for my family. However, when it came to sweets, I noticed that a lot of recipes require one to two cups of refined sugar, and I felt uncomfortable feeding that much sugar to my kids.

Not wanting to deprive them of yummy treats, and be one of those mothers who always says, 'No, you can't have that', I decided to come up with my own recipes. I started to make biscuits, cakes and desserts with no butter, no white flour and no added sugar. After a lot of experimenting and taste testing, I was able to create recipes that tasted just as delicious as the traditional alternatives. My first cookbook, *Have Your Cake*, was published in April 2011, with sixty delicious recipes including muffins, biscuits, cakes, friands, tarts and other heavenly desserts.

I try to teach my children that they can still have delicious meals, and even treats, using healthy ingredients that are high in fibre, low in sugars and saturated fats, and don't have lots of preservatives, additives, and artificial flavours and colours.

For me, one important ingredient of a successful recipe is to have fun and enjoy making it. I always find that the more involved my children are in the preparation, the more likely they are to enjoy the end result. Include your kids, especially when baking. Let them pour in ingredients, do the mixing, and definitely let them lick the bowl. When my kids eat the mixture, I always know that the recipe is going to be a success.

It's also important, for me, that the recipes are quick and easy to prepare, and that the ingredients are familiar, easy to work with and accessible. All of the ingredients that I use are available from the supermarket; however, I am careful to avoid products that contain a lot of additives and preservatives (usually indicated by numbers on the ingredients list).

Have fun trying new foods, taste test along the way, and feel comfortable adjusting recipes to suit your dietary needs.

Emily

PANTRY LIST

To make the cooking process easier, I keep my pantry stocked with the main ingredients I use, so that they are always on hand. I also keep my freezer stocked with frozen raspberries, blueberries, peas and corn kernels. When shopping at the supermarket, I am always careful to avoid products that contain a lot of additives and preservatives (indicated by numbers on the ingredients list).

olive oil (mild in flavour)

rice bran oil

light soy sauce

dijon mustard

honey (yellow box or raw honey)

tinned tomatoes

tinned tuna

basmati rice

wholemeal (wholewheat) pasta or rice pasta

wholemeal (wholewheat) couscous

rye wraps

wholemeal (wholewheat) self-raising flour

wholemeal (wholewheat) plain flour

eggs (use 59g eggs)

desiccated coconut

oats

organic dried apricots

sultanas

70% dark chocolate

COOKING TIPS

The following cooking tips will ensure that your dish is a success every time.

All recipes are quick and easy to prepare.

1. Use olive oil when cooking at low temperatures or for dressings and dips. Use rice bran oil when cooking at high temperatures, because it has a high smoke point. Both oils are low in saturated fats and are trans fat free.

2. When cooking meals, measurements don't have to be precise, and it won't matter if your potato weighs 200g or 280g. For simplicity, most recipes may say 'use 2 medium potatoes' or refer to cup measurements rather than the exact weight in grams. When baking, however, it's always important to follow the exact measurements, otherwise your muffins or biscuits won't turn out correctly.

3. If the recipe uses honey, always make sure to dissolve it in the wet ingredients before adding the dry ingredients. Use two separate measuring cups: one for dry ingredients and one for wet ingredients. If you measure the honey after the rice bran oil, it will slide out easily.

4. When measuring flour or other dry ingredients, tap the measuring cup to disperse all the air pockets in the ingredients. If the recipe says '½', then measure exactly to that line on the cup. 1 cup is the equivalent of 250ml. For tablespoon or teaspoon measurements, always use measuring spoons. In Australia, 1 teaspoon is the equivalent of 5ml, and 1 tablespoon is 20ml or 4 teaspoons (some tablespoons overseas are 15ml or the equivalent of 3 teaspoons). Measure teaspoons and tablespoons flat, not heaped.

5. To prepare wholemeal (wholewheat) breadcrumbs, freeze left-over bread. Once frozen, allow the bread to thaw for 5 minutes, and then place it in a food processor until crumbs form. Place any remaining breadcrumbs in an airtight container and put it back into the freezer, ready for next time.

6. Oven temperatures vary! It is important to always keep an eye on what you are cooking, and to check that it is cooked at the end of the predicted cooking time. If you don't have a fan-forced oven, cook at the temperature indicated in the recipe; however, you may find that you need to cook your food for 5 to 10 minutes longer. Biscuits and muffins may need up to 5 minutes longer, and cakes up to 15 minutes longer than the indicated cooking time.

7. If a recipe says 'grate', use a grater or food processor. If the recipe says 'blend', use either a hand-held blender, a bench blender or a food processor. If the recipe says 'whisk', use a whisk, and if it says 'beat', use a hand-held electric beater.

snack time

These great snack ideas are invaluable for lunchboxes
or as after-school munchies.

When the tummies are rumbling, but it's not time for dinner yet,
a delicious snack will give your kids energy and keep them
satisfied without ruining their appetites.

Freeze muffins and slices individually so you can bake once a
week and still have a delicious snack ready to go.

hummus and vegetable sticks

SERVES 4 TO 6

hummus

1 cup (180g) cooked chickpeas (fresh or
   tinned)

1½ tablespoons lemon juice

1 small garlic clove

2 tablespoons hulled tahini

⅓ cup (80ml) olive oil

2 tablespoons water

salt

vegetable sticks

1 medium carrot

1 red pepper

2 celery sticks

1 Lebanese cucumber

- Place the cooked chickpeas (if using tinned chickpeas, rinse and drain well), lemon juice, garlic, tahini, olive oil, water and salt in a food processor and blend until smooth.

- Slice the carrot, pepper, celery and cucumber and serve with the hummus.

- Store any left over hummus in an airtight container and refrigerate.

NOTE: Hummus is also great as a spread on wholemeal toast.

12

avocado dip with toasted pita bites

SERVES 4 TO 6

avocado dip

2 boiled eggs

1 avocado

2 teaspoons mayonnaise

salt

toasted pita bites

3 wholemeal (wholewheat) pitas

1 tablespoon rice bran oil

1 garlic clove, crushed

1 teaspoon dried oregano leaves

- Preheat oven to 200°C (390°F) fan-forced.

- Place the boiled eggs, avocado, mayonnaise and salt in a bowl, and mash with a fork. Taste and add more salt if needed.

- Using scissors, cut pitas in half and then into triangles. Place oil and garlic in a bowl. Line a baking tray with baking paper and place pita triangles on the tray. Brush each triangle with oil and sprinkle with some oregano leaves.

- Bake for 6 to 8 minutes.

14

cheese melts

SERVES 2

4 slices rye bread

2 medium tomatoes, sliced

200g bocconcini cheese, sliced

extra virgin olive oil for drizzling

- Preheat oven grill on medium heat.

- Lightly toast the rye bread in toaster.

- Place tomato on toast, and top with bocconcini.

- Grill for 2 to 3 minutes or until cheese melts. Drizzle with olive oil.

tuna wrap rolls

SERVES 2

160g tuna (tinned)

3 teaspoons mayonnaise

½ continental cucumber

½ avocado

2 rye wraps

- Place the tuna and mayonnaise in a bowl and mash with a fork.

- Slice the cucumber lengthways into strips and remove the seeds. Slice the avocado.

- Place the rye wrap on a sushi mat to assist in rolling the wrap firmly. Place tuna in the centre, then top with cucumber and avocado. Roll the wrap and then slice.

anzac biscuits

MAKES 16 TO 20

1 cup (100g) rolled oats

¾ cup (75g) desiccated coconut

1 cup (160g) wholemeal (wholewheat)
    plain flour

1½ teaspoons bicarbonate of soda

2 tablespoons boiling water

½ cup (150g) honey

½ cup (125ml) rice bran oil

- Preheat oven to 150°C (300°F) fan-forced.

- Mix the rolled oats, coconut and flour together. In a separate bowl, dissolve the bicarbonate of soda with the boiling water, and mix in the oil and honey until smooth. Add the liquid to the dry ingredients and mix with a spoon.

- Line two trays with baking paper and roll mixture into balls, or use two teaspoons to scoop the mixture onto the trays.

- Bake for 20 minutes.

- Remove from oven and place biscuits on a wire rack to cool.

chocolate oat cookies

MAKES 18

1 egg

½ cup (125ml) rice bran oil

½ cup (150g) honey

¼ cup (60ml) water

1 tablespoon cocoa powder

½ cup (50g) desiccated coconut

½ cup (50g) rolled oats

1¼ cups (200g) wholemeal (wholewheat) self-raising flour

⅓ cup (45g) finely chopped 70% dark chocolate

- Preheat oven to 160°C (315°F) fan-forced.

- Mix the egg and oil together. Add honey and water, and mix until dissolved. Add cocoa powder.

- Stir in the coconut, oats and flour until combined, and then add the chopped chocolate. Mix with a spoon.

- Leave mixture to stand for 5 minutes to become less sticky, then roll into small balls and flatten between the palms of your hands. Line tray with baking paper, then place the cookies on the tray.

- Bake for 20 minutes.

- Remove from oven and place cookies on a wire rack to cool.

cranberry and coconut muesli bars

MAKES 16

1½ cups (150g) rolled oats

1¼ cups (125g) desiccated coconut

1 tablespoon sesame seeds

½ teaspoon cinnamon

½ cup (70g) dried cranberries

½ cup (70g) sultanas

½ cup (150g) honey

1 tablespoon water

⅓ cup (80ml) rice bran oil

2 egg whites

- Preheat oven to 160°C (315°F) fan-forced.

- Mix together the oats, coconut, sesame seeds, cinnamon, cranberries and sultanas.

- In a separate bowl, mix together the honey, water and oil until honey dissolves. Add to the dry ingredients. Mix in egg whites until combined.

- Grease a brownie tin (28 cm x 18 cm) with oil, and line the base with baking paper. Press the mixture firmly into the tin.

- Bake for 35 minutes.

- Remove from oven. While hot and still in the tin, use a sharp (non-serrated) knife and slice the cake into 16 even bars. Leave to cool in the tin for at least 10 to 15 minutes before removing each bar with a lifter. Line a tray with baking paper, turn the muesli bars upside down and bake for a further 5 minutes.

- Remove from oven and leave to cool on a wire rack.

fruit muffins

MAKES 12

2 eggs

½ cup (125ml) rice bran oil

½ cup (150g) honey

½ cup (50g) desiccated coconut

1½ cups (240g) wholemeal (wholewheat)
   self-raising flour

½ cup (125ml) orange juice

⅓ cup (55g) dried figs, diced

⅓ cup (50g) dried apricots, diced

⅓ cup (50g) dried sultanas

1 tablespoon rolled oats

- Preheat oven to 170°C (335°F) fan-forced.

- Whisk eggs and oil together until fluffy. Mix in honey.

- Add coconut, flour and orange juice, and whisk until combined.

- Mix the figs, apricots, and sultanas into the mixture.

- Grease muffin tin with oil, and fill each muffin case with mixture ¾ full. Sprinkle some oats over the top of each muffin.

- Bake for 20 minutes.

- Leave to cool for 10 minutes before removing the muffins from the tin and placing them on a wire rack to cool further.

27

oat slice

MAKES 15

2 eggs

½ cup (125ml) rice bran oil

½ cup (150g) honey

½ cup (80g) wholemeal (wholewheat)
   self-raising flour

1 cup (100g) oats

1 cup (100g) desiccated coconut

- Preheat oven to 170°C (335°F) fan-forced.

- Whisk eggs, oil and honey together until smooth. Use a spoon to stir in the flour, oats and coconut.

- Grease a brownie tray (28 cm x 18 cm) with rice bran oil and line base with baking paper. Spread the mixture evenly over the tin.

- Bake for 20 minutes.

- Leave to cool for 10 minutes before removing from the tin and placing on a wire rack to cool further.

blueberry slice

MAKES 15

3 eggs

⅓ cup (80ml) rice bran oil

⅓ cup (95g) honey

½ cup (50g) desiccated coconut

1 cup (160g) wholemeal (wholewheat)
   self-raising flour

⅓ cup (80ml) orange juice

½ cup (65g) blueberries (fresh or frozen)

- Preheat oven to 160°C (315°F) fan-forced.

- Whisk together eggs and oil until fluffy. Add honey and mix until dissolved.

- Mix in coconut and flour. Add orange juice and combine.

- Grease a brownie tin (28 cm x 18 cm) with oil and line base with baking paper. Pour mixture into the tin. Place blueberries evenly over the top of the mixture.

- Bake for 25 minutes.

- Remove from oven and allow to cool for 20 minutes before removing the cake from the tin and placing it on a wire rack to cool further. Once cooled, slice.

meals

These recipes are quick to prepare, easy to make, and combine all the yummy foods kids love to eat.

When cooking, exact measurements aren't critical, and your dish will taste just as delicious whether your potato weighs 300g or 400g. For simplicity, these recipes refer to mainly cup measurements, and use terms such as 'medium' or 'large' when referring to the size of ingredients, rather than state their exact weight.

Have fun, taste test along the way and feel comfortable making changes to the recipe to satisfy your own palate.

chicken schnitzel

SERVES 4

4 chicken breast fillets, butterflied

3 tablespoons wholemeal (wholewheat) plain flour

2 eggs, whisked

2 cups wholemeal (wholewheat) breadcrumbs

rice bran oil for frying

- Slice each chicken breast into 3 pieces and thin with a meat mallet.

- Place flour, eggs and breadcrumbs in separate bowls. Dip each chicken piece into the flour, then into the whisked eggs and cover with breadcrumbs (for preparation of breadcrumbs, see cooking tips, page 8).

- Pour oil into a large frying pan until the base of pan is covered (approximately 2 ml). Heat on high flame and place crumbed chicken in pan. When the schnitzel begins to brown around the edges (3 to 4 minutes), turn over and reduce heat to medium to cook the chicken through.

- When cooked, place the chicken on kitchen paper to soak up any excess oil.

- Serve with sweet potato mash (see page 68).

34

steak in wraps

SERVES 4

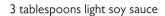

3 tablespoons light soy sauce

1 teaspoon honey

1 teaspoon dijon mustard

4 steaks

2 medium tomatoes

1 cucumber

1 avocado

4 rye wraps

- Preheat oven grill on high.

- Place soy sauce, honey and mustard in a dish and mix. Add steak and marinate.

- Place steaks on a tray in oven and grill each side for 3 to 4 minutes, depending on how well you like your meat cooked.

- Slice steak, removing any fat.

- Slice tomatoes, cucumber and avocado.

- To prepare wraps, place tomato, cucumber, avocado and steak slices in the centre, fold up the bottom of the wrap and then fold to enclose the filling.

fish nuggets

SERVES 4

4 flathead fillets (skinned and boned)

3 tablespoons wholemeal (wholewheat) plain flour

2 eggs, whisked

2 cups wholemeal (wholewheat) breadcrumbs

rice bran oil for frying

- Slice flathead into nuggets, approximately 6 cm long.

- Place flour, eggs and breadcrumbs in individual bowls. Dip each fish nugget into flour, then into the eggs and cover with breadcrumbs (for preparation of breadcrumbs, see cooking tips, page 8).

- Pour oil into large frying pan until the base of pan is covered (approximately 2 ml). Heat on high flame and place fish in pan. When the fish nuggets begin to brown around the edges (2 to 3 minutes), turn over and reduce heat to medium.

- When they are cooked, place the nuggets on kitchen paper to remove any excess oil.

- Serve with veggie chips (see page 70).

pasta with napoli sauce

SERVES 4

1 garlic clove, crushed

1 medium brown onion, diced

1 tablespoon rice bran oil

800g tinned tomatoes

1 tablespoon chopped fresh basil,
    and extra for serving

salt and pepper

280g penne rice pasta (uncooked)

- Crush garlic and finely dice onion. Place oil in saucepan, add garlic and onion, and cook on medium to high heat for a few minutes.

- Blend tomatoes and add to saucepan along with the basil. Season with salt and pepper.

- Bring to boil, then reduce heat to low and simmer for 45 minutes. Taste and add salt if needed.

- Cook pasta in large saucepan of salted, boiling water until just tender. Drain and add desired amount of napoli sauce to serve.

- Serve with fresh basil.

pizza

SERVES 2 TO 4

8 tablespoons napoli sauce (see page 41)

2 pieces wholemeal (wholewheat)
 Lebanese flatbread

180g bocconcini cheese

handful basil leaves

- Preheat oven to 200°C (390°F) fan-forced.

- Spread 4 tablespoons of napoli sauce over the base of each flatbread.

- Using your fingers, crumble the bocconcini on top of the sauce. Place a few leaves of fresh basil on top.

- Add your favourite toppings (see note).

- Cook for 10 minutes.

NOTE: Now you have your base, you can add a variety of toppings, such as olives, capsicum, mushrooms, avocado, pineapple or cherry tomatoes.

42

spinach and mushroom lasagne

SERVES 6

1 tablespoon rice bran oil

380g button mushrooms, sliced

1 garlic clove, finely chopped

2 eggs

500g spinach (frozen, allow to thaw)

250g ricotta

salt

1½ cups (380g) napoli sauce (see page 41)

250g wholemeal (wholewheat)
   lasagne sheets

90g bocconcini

- Preheat oven to 180°C (350°F) fan-forced.

- Place oil in frying pan on high heat. Add mushrooms and garlic to the pan, and lower heat to medium. Stir occasionally with a wooden spoon until cooked (approximately 2 to 3 minutes).

- To prepare the spinach mix, place eggs in a bowl and whisk. Drain spinach, then add to eggs along with the ricotta and salt. Mix thoroughly.

- Place a small amount of napoli sauce over the base of the dish (24 cm x 22 cm), then cover with lasagne sheets.

- Spread half of the spinach mix over the lasagne sheets, then add another layer of lasagne sheets.

continued on page 46

44

- Top with some napoli sauce and place the mushrooms on top. Add another layer of lasagne sheets followed by the remaining spinach mix.

- Place the final layer of lasagne sheets on top and cover with the rest of the napoli sauce. Make sure that the pasta is completely covered. Using your fingers, crumble bocconcini over the top.

- Cover with foil and place in oven.

- Bake for 40 minutes, then remove foil and bake for a further 10 minutes.

honey soy drumsticks

SERVES 6

3 tablespoons honey

100ml light soy sauce

1 garlic clove, crushed

½ lemon

12 chicken drumsticks

- Preheat oven to 180°C (350°F) fan-forced.

- Place honey, soy sauce, garlic and juice of half a lemon in a dish and mix until smooth. Add chicken and cover each piece with sauce. Marinate for 2 to 3 hours or overnight in the refrigerator.

- Line a baking tray with foil and place drumsticks on tray.

- Cook for 50 minutes, turning the pieces over after 30 minutes.

- Serve with plain basmati rice or fried rice (see page 74).

49

lamb chops

SERVES 4

4 tablespoons light soy sauce

2 teaspoons honey

12 to 16 lamb chops

- Preheat oven grill on high.

- Place soy sauce and honey in a dish and mix. Cover chops in sauce and marinate for 2 to 3 hours in refrigerator.

- Cover a tray with foil and place chops on the tray. Grill each side for about 3 minutes, depending on how well you like your meat cooked.

- Serve with stir-fry vegetables (see page 72).

50

tuna pasta

SERVES 4

360g wholemeal (wholewheat) spaghetti
(uncooked)
1 teaspoon rice bran oil
1 garlic clove, finely chopped
100g cherry tomatoes
160g tinned tuna (drained)
2 teaspoons capers
4 tablespoons olive oil
1 tablespoon pasta water

- Cook pasta in salted, boiling water until tender. Before draining the pasta, set aside 1 tablespoon of pasta water for the sauce.

- Place rice bran oil in frying pan on high heat. Add garlic and cook until lightly brown. Reduce heat to low. Cut tomatoes in half, squeeze out the juice into the frying pan and then toss in tomatoes.

- Mix in the tuna and capers, and cook for 2 minutes. Turn heat off, mix in olive oil and add the reserved pasta water.

- Toss the cooked spaghetti through the sauce and serve.

52

chicken patties

MAKES 8 TO 10

2 tablespoons rice bran oil for frying

1 small brown onion, finely diced

1 egg

½ teaspoon dried rosemary flakes

½ cup wholemeal (wholewheat)
    breadcrumbs

salt and pepper

600g chicken mince (mixture of thigh
    and breast meat)

- Preheat oven to 160°C (315°F) fan-forced.

- Heat frying pan with 1 tablespoon of oil on medium to high heat and cook onions until brown.

- In a bowl, mix egg, rosemary flakes, breadcrumbs, and season with salt and pepper (for preparation of breadcrumbs, see cooking tips, page 8).

- Add the cooked onions and chicken mince to the bowl, and mix thoroughly using your hands.

- Heat frying pan on medium to high heat with the remaining oil. Shape the mince into balls and flatten between your palms. Place patties in frying pan and brown each side (approximately 2 to 3 minutes per side).

- Place patties in a dish and cook in oven for a further 15 to 20 minutes.

- Serve with rosemary and garlic potatoes (see page 78).

hamburger

SERVES 4

beef pattie

4 teaspoons rice bran oil

1 small brown onion, finely diced

1 egg

2 teaspoons dijon mustard

2 teaspoons light soy sauce

⅓ cup wholemeal (wholewheat) breadcrumbs

500g beef mince

toppings

1 tablespoon rice bran oil

1 large brown onion, sliced

4 wholemeal (wholewheat) bread rolls

4 lettuce leaves (cos or iceberg lettuce)

2 medium tomatoes, sliced

mayonnaise

- Preheat oven to 180°C (350°F) fan-forced.

- Heat frying pan with 2 teaspoons of oil on medium to high heat and cook the diced onion until brown.

- In a bowl, mix egg, mustard and soy sauce. Add breadcrumbs, mince and cooked onion, and mix thoroughly (for preparation of breadcrumbs, see cooking tips, page 8).

- Heat frying pan with 2 teaspoons of oil on medium to high heat. Make mince into balls and flatten between your palms to make 4 patties (½ cup each). Place in frying pan and brown each side (approximately 2 to 3 minutes per side).

- Place the patties in a baking dish and cook for a further 15 minutes in the oven.

continued on page 58

- Cook the sliced onion in a frying pan with 1 tablespoon of oil until brown.

- To prepare the hamburger, spread some mayonnaise over the base of the roll, add the lettuce, tomato, beef pattie, and top with onions.

beef skewers

SERVES 4

2 tablespoons light soy sauce

1 tablespoon honey

2 teaspoons balsamic vinegar

500g scotch fillet or eye fillet, cubed

1 red capsicum, cubed

1 green capsicum, cubed

8 bamboo skewers

- Heat oven grill on high.

- To prepare marinade, mix the soy sauce, honey and balsamic vinegar in a bowl until smooth. Add the meat and leave to marinate in refrigerator for 1 to 2 hours.

- Soak bamboo skewers in water for an hour to prevent them from burning when grilling.

- Alternately arrange meat, and red and green capsicum on each skewer, ending with a piece of meat.

- Cover a tray with silver foil, place skewer on tray and grill each side for 3 minutes (or to your liking).

crumbed chicken and salsa in pita

SERVES 4

crumbed chicken

2 chicken fillets, butterflied

1½ cups wholemeal (wholewheat)
     breadcrumbs

1 teaspoon mild paprika

salt

salsa

1 avocado, diced

1 cucumber, peeled and diced

2 tomatoes, diced

1½ tablespoons lemon juice

1 tablespoon olive oil

salt

4 wholemeal (wholewheat) pitas

mayonnaise

- Preheat oven to 180°C (350°F) fan-forced.

- Slice chicken into nuggets, approximately 4 cm long. Place breadcrumbs, paprika and a pinch of salt in a bowl and mix (for preparation of breadcrumbs, see cooking tips, page 8).

- Dip chicken nuggets into breadcrumbs until coated. Line a baking tray with foil and place nuggets on tray.

- Cook for 25 minutes.

- To prepare salsa, gently combine avocado, cucumber and tomatoes in a bowl. Toss with lemon juice, oil and salt to taste.

- To warm pitas, wrap in foil and place in oven for 2 to 3 minutes.

- To serve, slice the pitas in half, spread some mayonnaise over the base of the pita, and top with chicken nuggets and salsa.

62

sticky lamb ribs

SERVES 4

3 tablespoons honey

4 tablespoons light soy sauce

2 dozen lamb ribs

- Preheat oven to 180°C (350°F) fan-forced.

- Place honey and soy sauce in a dish, and mix until smooth. Toss lamb ribs in sauce and leave to marinate for a few hours in the refrigerator.

- Line a baking tray with foil and place ribs on tray.

- Cook for 30 to 35 minutes or until brown.

- Serve with green beans or vegetable fritters (see page 77).

sides

These side dishes are a great way to get a variety of vegetables into your kids. Simply choose a delicious, healthy side to serve with a main meal.

sweet potato mash

SERVES 4 TO 6

2 medium sweet potatoes, cubed

1 medium potato, cubed

1 small garlic clove, peeled

salt

1 tablespoon olive oil

- Place sweet potato, potato and garlic in a saucepan filled with approximately 2 cm of water. Bring to the boil, then reduce heat to simmer. Add pinch of salt to the water.

- When cooked (approximately 30 minutes; use a fork to test whether vegetables are soft), drain water, add oil and mash until smooth. Season with salt.

veggie chips

SERVES 4 TO 6

3 large potatoes

1 medium sweet potato

1 medium carrot

1 tablespoon rice bran oil

salt

- Preheat oven to 180°C (350°F) fan-forced.

- Peel potatoes, sweet potato and carrot, and slice into sticks. Place in a bowl, toss with oil and season with salt.

- Place on a tray and cook for 45 minutes or until golden.

stir-fry vegetables

SERVES 4 TO 6

1 tablespoon rice bran oil

180g broccoli

100g snowpeas

100g sugar snaps

100g green beans

150g button mushrooms, sliced

1 tablespoon light soy sauce

- Cut broccoli into pieces, and cut off the ends of the snowpeas, sugar snaps and beans.

- Place oil in a large non-stick frying pan or wok, and heat on medium heat. Add broccoli first and cook for a few minutes. Then add the snowpeas, sugar snaps, beans and mushrooms.

- Add soy sauce and toss the vegetables. Cook for 3 to 4 minutes until tender but still crisp. If needed, add a little water while cooking.

fried rice

SERVES 6

4 cups cooked basmati rice

2 teaspoons rice bran oil for frying

2 spring onions, finely sliced

200g button mushrooms, sliced

¾ cup corn kernels (fresh or frozen)

¾ cup peas (fresh or frozen)

1 tablespoon light soy sauce

1 egg

- Cook rice and set aside to cool.

- Heat frying pan or wok on high heat and add oil and spring onions.

- Cook onions for a few minutes until they begin to soften, and then add mushrooms. If using frozen corn and peas, allow to thaw and then add to frying pan.

- Add soy sauce. Cook vegetables for 3 to 4 minutes.

- Whisk egg and, in a separate frying pan, make an omelette. When cooked, use the top of a lifter to slice the egg into small pieces.

- Add rice and egg to vegetables and gently combine all ingredients.

vegetable fritters

MAKES 10 TO 12

1 medium carrot

1 medium zucchini

2 medium potatoes

½ cup corn kernels, cooked (fresh
   or frozen)

4 teaspoons rice bran oil

½ small red onion, finely diced

2 eggs

¼ cup wholemeal (wholewheat)
   self-raising flour

½ cup wholemeal (wholewheat)
   breadcrumbs

salt

- Preheat oven to 160°C (315°F) fan-forced.

- Grate carrot, zucchini and potatoes, and place in a bowl. Add cooked corn kernels (if using frozen kernels, allow to thaw).

- Add 2 teaspoons of oil to the frying pan and heat on medium to high heat. Add onions and cook until brown.

- In a bowl, combine the eggs, flour and breadcrumbs (for preparation of breadcrumbs, see cooking tips, page 8). Add pinch of salt. Mix in vegetables and onion.

- Heat frying pan with the remaining oil on high heat. Make mixture into balls and squeeze out any excess juice into the bowl. Slightly flatten the balls between your palms and place in frying pan. Brown fritters evenly on both sides (approximately 2 to 3 minutes on each side).

- Place fritters in a dish and cook for a further 25 minutes in oven.

rosemary and garlic potatoes
SERVES 4

12 chat potatoes

1 tablespoon rice bran oil

salt

3 garlic cloves

2 sprigs rosemary leaves

- Preheat oven to 180°C (350°F) fan-forced.

- Wash and dry potatoes, then slice into quarters. Place in a bowl with oil, season with salt and toss.

- Line a baking tray with baking paper and spread potatoes over the tray. Place garlic cloves on the tray, and rest sprigs of rosemary on top of the potatoes.

- Cook for 1 hour, tossing potatoes after 30 minutes.

- Before serving, discard garlic cloves and rosemary.

78

chopped salad
SERVES 4 TO 6

salad

1 medium carrot, peeled and diced

1 cucumber, peeled and diced

1 red capsicum, diced

2 celery sticks, diced

1 avocado, diced

dressing

¼ cup olive oil

¼ cup white wine vinegar

2 teaspoons dijon mustard

salt

- Place all of the salad ingredients in a bowl, and toss gently with desired amount of dressing.

- To prepare dressing, place ingredients in a jar and shake well. Store remaining dressing in refrigerator.

couscous and vegetables

SERVES 4

220g pumpkin, cubed

220g sweet potato, cubed

1 tablespoon rice bran oil

1 ½ cups (375ml) chicken stock

1½ cups wholemeal (wholeweat) couscous

2 tablespoons olive oil

½ cup cooked peas (fresh or frozen)

- Preheat oven to 180°C (350°F) fan-forced.

- Toss the pumpkin and sweet potato with rice bran oil.

- Place on a tray and cook for 30 minutes.

- Place chicken stock in a saucepan on high heat. When stock begins to bubble, turn heat off and add couscous and olive oil. Stir briefly, then place lid over the saucepan to keep the heat in. Leave lid on for 10 minutes, then fluff with a fork. Cover with lid for a further 5 minutes.

- Place couscous in a bowl and toss with pumpkin, sweet potato and peas.

82

fruit snacks

There are lots of ways to make fruit fun and exciting for your kids, and they don't take too much time to prepare.

I always find that the more involved my kids are in the preparation, the more likely they are to eat what I serve them. My daughter loves to prepare fruit for the family and decorate the plate, making it difficult to resist what's being served.

banana split

SERVES 2

banana ice-cream

1 banana

¾ cup (180g) natural yoghurt

1 tablespoon honey

banana split

2 bananas

2 scoops banana ice-cream

40g 70% dark chocolate, melted

2 raspberries for decorating

- Blend together banana, yoghurt and honey until smooth. Place in an airtight container and freeze for at least 6 hours, (can be prepared the day before serving).

- Slice banana in half lengthways. Place a scoop of ice-cream in the centre. Drizzle with melted chocolate and place a raspberry on top.

berry blast

SERVES 2

½ cup (65g) blueberries

½ cup (65g) raspberries

5 (90g) strawberries

½ cup (120g) natural yoghurt

1 tablespoon honey

8 (80g) ice cubes

- Blend blueberries, raspberries and strawberries together. If using frozen berries, allow to thaw slightly before blending.

- Add yoghurt and honey, and blend until mixed in.

- Add ice and blend.

fruit icy poles

MAKES 4 TO 5

350g pineapple, cored and cubed

⅔ cup (165ml) orange juice

¼ (60ml) cup water

16 to 20 raspberries

- Blend pineapple, then add orange juice and water.

- Fill 4 to 5 icy pole containers with juice and add 4 raspberries to each. Leave to set in the freezer for at least 5 hours.

90

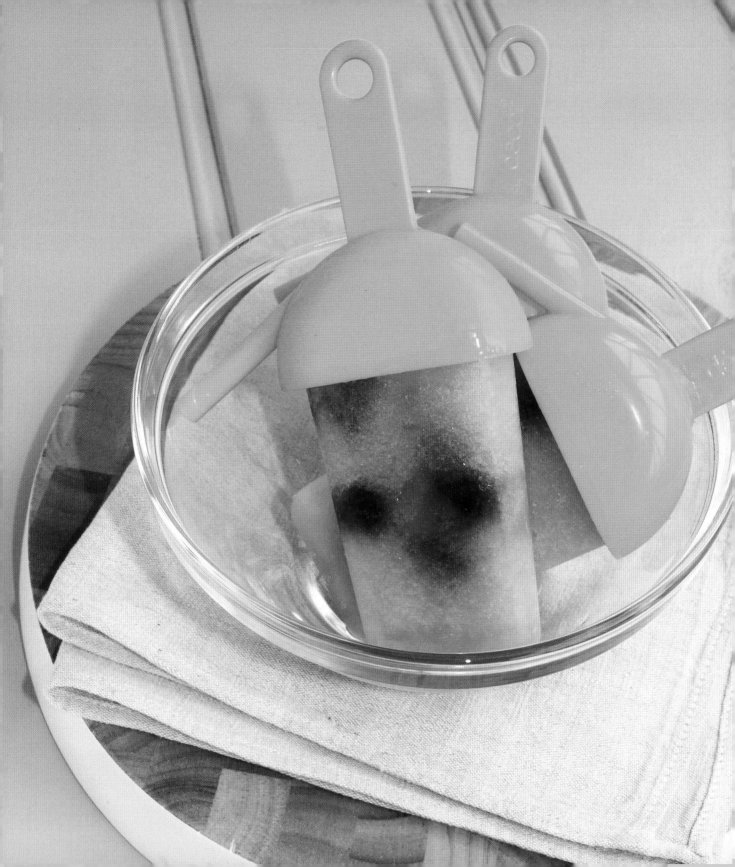

fruit cups with yoghurt and chocolate

SERVES 2

2 slices watermelon

4 strawberries

1 banana

12 grapes

1 apple, diced

2 dessertspoons yoghurt

2 tablespoons orange juice

70% dark chocolate, grated,
   for decoration

- Cut watermelon, strawberries and banana into small pieces. Cut grapes in half. Add apple.

- Divide the fruit into two cups, top with a dessertspoon of yoghurt and add a tablespoon of orange juice. Finish with some grated chocolate.

93

watermelon and mango slushies

200g watermelon

1 mango

200g ice

- Blend watermelon and mango flesh. Add ice and blend.

fruit skewers

MAKES 6

6 cubes (110g) rockmelon

6 strawberries

12 cubes (220g) pineapple

6 cubes (110g) honeydew melon

6 cubes (110g) watermelon

6 bamboo skewers

- To assemble, place a piece of rockmelon, strawberry, pineapple, honeydew melon, watermelon and, lastly, another piece of pineapple on each skewer.

96

mango sorbet
SERVES 4

1.5 mangoes

1 tablespoon honey

1 tablespoon boiling water

2 tablespoons orange juice

2 egg whites

- Remove the skin and seed from the mangoes and blend until smooth (if using frozen mangoes, allow to thaw). Dissolve the honey in the boiling water and mix into the mangoes. Add orange juice and mix.

- In a separate bowl, beat egg whites until stiff.

- Gently fold egg whites into mango mixture until combined.

- Place the mango sorbet in an airtight container and freeze. Prepare the day before serving, to allow the sorbet to freeze.

pineapple granita

SERVES 4

350g pineapple, sliced and cored

¼ cup orange juice

1 cup water

- Blend pineapple. Add orange juice and water. Strain mixture (optional), then pour into a lamington tin and freeze.

- After 2 hours, use a fork to scrape the granita mix and break it up into small ice crystals. Repeat this procedure two more times with 1 hour freezing in between, before serving.

melon boat

SERVES 2

120g watermelon

120g rockmelon

120g honeydew melon

- Using a melon baller, scoop watermelon, rockmelon and honeydew melon to make melon balls (approximately 8 for each fruit).

- Slice 2 thick portions from the base of the watermelon and hollow them out to create 'boats' for the melon balls.

102

birthday party treats

You can still serve an irresistible table full of treats at your child's party and keep all your guests happy, without having them running around in circles after eating lots of party food.

With no preservatives, additives, artificial flavourings and colourings and, of course, no added sugar, you can feel comfortable serving these delicious treats to your children and their friends.

Select four or five treats, depending on the number of guests, and you will be able to make the perfect party table for your child.

lemon cupcakes with passionfruit icing

MAKES 12

2 eggs

½ (125ml) cup rice bran oil

½ cup (150g) honey

5 tablespoons lemon juice

3 tablespoons desiccated coconut

1½ cups (240g) wholemeal
(wholewheat) self-raising flour

2 tablespoons milk

icing

¼ cup (60g) ricotta

2 tablespoons honey

1 teaspoon rice bran oil

½ cup (50g) desiccated coconut

2 teaspoons orange juice

1 passionfruit

- Preheat oven to 170°C (335°F) fan-forced.

- Beat eggs, oil and honey together. Add lemon juice and coconut. Mix in flour and milk.

- Line a cupcake tin with patty cases and fill each case until ¾ full with mixture.

- Bake for 18 minutes.

- Leave the cupcakes in the tin for 5 minutes before transferring to a wire rack to cool.

- To prepare the icing, place the ricotta, honey, oil, coconut and orange juice in a food processor and blend. Using a spoon, mix in the pulp of one passionfruit. Spoon icing over the cupcakes.

- Store in refrigerator.

vanilla cupcakes with chocolate icing

MAKES 12

2 eggs

½ cup (125ml) rice bran oil

½ cup (150g) honey

1 vanilla bean

1½ cups (240g) wholemeal (wholewheat)
    self-raising flour

⅓ cup (80ml) milk

icing

60g 70% dark chocolate

1 tablespoon honey

- Preheat oven to 170°C (335°F) fan-forced.

- Beat eggs, oil and honey together. Slice vanilla
  bean lengthways and, using a knife, scrape
  out seeds and add to mixture. Use the back of
  a spoon to rub the vanilla bean seeds against
  the side of the bowl to allow the seeds to
  dissolve evenly into the mixture. Mix in the
  flour and milk.

- Line a cupcake tin with patty cases and fill
  each case until ¾ full with mixture.

- Bake for 18 minutes.

- Leave the cupcakes in the tin for 5 minutes
  before transferring to a wire rack to cool.

- To prepare the icing, melt the chocolate, add
  honey, and mix until smooth. Spoon icing over
  the cupcakes.

birthday cake

MAKES 12

4 eggs, separated

1 cup (250ml) rice bran oil

¾ cup (225g) honey

1 vanilla bean

1 teaspoon bicarbonate of soda

1 tablespoon boiling water

½ cup (50g) desiccated coconut

2 cups (320g) wholemeal (wholewheat)
   self-raising flour

½ cup (125ml) orange juice

100g 70% dark chocolate

icing

120g 70% dark chocolate

2 tablespoons honey

2 teaspoons rice bran oil

6 tablespoons 100% strawberry jam

- Preheat oven to 160°C (315°F) fan-forced.

- Beat egg whites until stiff.

- In a separate bowl, mix together the yolks, oil and honey until smooth, then add vanilla bean seeds. To extract seeds, slice vanilla bean lengthways and, using a knife, scrape out seeds. Using the back of a spoon, rub the vanilla bean seeds against the side of the bowl to allow the seeds to dissolve evenly into the mixture.

- Dissolve bicarbonate of soda in the boiling water and add to yolk mixture. Mix in coconut, flour and orange juice.

- Pour half of the yolk mixture into another bowl. Melt dark chocolate, add to one of the bowls and mix in thoroughly.

continued on page 113

- Take half of the egg whites (divide with a spatula) and gently fold into the vanilla mixture until combined. Add the remaining egg whites to the chocolate mixture and fold in until combined.

- Grease two round tins (20 cm) with oil and line base with baking paper.

- Pour vanilla mixture into one and the chocolate mixture into the other. Bake for 35 minutes (both tins should fit on the same shelf).

- Allow cakes to cool for 20 minutes before removing from tin, then leave cakes on wire racks to cool further.

- To prepare the icing, melt chocolate, and stir in honey and oil until smooth.

- Carefully slice each cake horizontally in half. Place a layer of chocolate cake on a plate and spread 2 tablespoons of jam over the top. Place a layer of vanilla cake on top and cover with 2 tablespoons of jam. Repeat the process for the final two layers. Spread the chocolate icing over the top and sides of the cake.

jam surprise muffins

MAKES 12

2 eggs

½ cup (150g) honey

½ cup (125ml) rice bran oil

1½ cups (240g) wholemeal
   (wholewheat) self-raising flour

½ cup (50g) desiccated coconut

⅔ cup (165ml) milk

cinnamon for dusting

½ cup 100% strawberry jam

- Preheat oven to 170°C (335°F) fan-forced.

- Beat eggs, honey and oil together. Add flour and coconut. Mix in milk.

- Grease each muffin tin with oil, and use a strainer to dust the tin with cinnamon.

- Fill each muffin tin ⅓ full with mixture, and place 1 teaspoon of strawberry jam into the centre of the mixture of each muffin. Add remaining mixture, filling each one ⅔ full. Dust the top with cinnamon.

- Bake for 20 minutes.

- Leave the muffins in the tin for 10 minutes before transfering to a wire rack to cool.

orange and chocolate swirl cakes

MAKES 10

2 eggs

½ cup (125ml) and 2 teaspoons rice
   bran oil

½ cup (150g) honey

1 teaspoon finely grated orange rind

⅓ cup (80ml) orange juice

2 tablespoons desiccated coconut

1½ cups (240g) wholemeal
   (wholewheat) self-raising flour

1 tablespoon water

2 tablespoons milk

60g 70% dark chocolate

- Preheat oven to 170°C (335°F) fan-forced.

- Whisk together eggs and ½ cup of oil. Mix in honey, orange rind and orange juice.

- Mix in coconut and flour. Add water and milk, and whisk until combined.

- Melt chocolate and combine with the remaining oil.

- Grease a friand tin with oil, and fill each case ⅓ full with mixture. Using a teaspoon, swirl some of the chocolate mixture over the top. Add the remaining cake mixture, filling each friand case ⅔ full. Swirl the remaining chocolate over the top.

- Bake for 18 to 20 minutes.

- Leave the friands in the tin for 20 minutes before transferring to a wire rack to cool.

chocolate crunches

MAKES 20

1 cup (100g) rolled oats

4 tablespoons honey

1 tablespoon boiling water

¾ cup (75g) desiccated coconut

120g 70% dark chocolate

- Preheat oven to 160°C (315°F) fan-forced.

- Place oats in a bowl. In a separate bowl, dissolve 2 tablespoons of honey in water, then mix into the oats. Line a tray with baking paper and spread oats over the tray. Bake for 15 minutes, tossing halfway through.

- Remove from oven and allow to cool.

- Place toasted oats and coconut in a bowl and mix.

- Melt chocolate, and mix in the remaining honey into the chocolate until dissolved. Mix chocolate mixture thoroughly into oat mixture.

- Scoop dollops of mixture into mini patty cases (patty cases can be placed in mini muffin tins) and refrigerate for 1 hour or until set.

jam and coconut slice

MAKES 16 TO 20

base

2 egg yolks

⅓ (80ml) rice bran oil

⅓ cup (95g) honey

½ cup (50g) desiccated coconut

¾ cup (120g) wholemeal (wholewheat)
   self-raising flour

topping

2 egg whites

1 tablespoon honey

½ cup (50g) desiccated coconut

⅓ cup (95g) 100% strawberry jam

- Preheat oven to 160°C (315°F) fan-forced.

- To prepare the base, use a spoon to mix together egg yolks, oil and honey. Mix in coconut and flour until combined.

- Grease a brownie tin (28 cm x 18 cm) with oil, and line base with baking paper. Use the back of a spoon to spread the mixture evenly over the base (it will be a thin layer). Bake for 10 minutes.

- While base is baking, prepare topping. Beat egg whites until stiff, then mix in the honey. Fold in coconut until combined.

- When base is ready, remove from oven and use a blunt knife to spread the jam over the top. Using a spatula, spread the coconut topping over the jam. Bake for a further 15 minutes.

- Remove from oven and leave to cool for 20 minutes before removing the cake from the tin. Once cooled, slice.

121

strawberry cupcakes
MAKES 12

2 eggs

½ cup (125ml) rice bran oil

½ cup (150g) honey

200g strawberries

1 tablespoon boiling water

½ cup (50g) desiccated coconut

1½ cups (240g) wholemeal
(wholewheat) self-raising flour

⅓ cup (80ml) milk

icing

¼ cup (60g) ricotta

2 tablespoons honey

1 teaspoon rice bran oil

½ cup (50g) desiccated coconut

2 teaspoons orange juice

3 strawberries, sliced into quarters

- Preheat oven to 170°C (335°F) fan-forced.

- Beat together eggs and oil until fluffy. Mix in honey until dissolved.

- Blend strawberries and boiling water until smooth, then add to mixture.

- Add coconut and flour, and then mix in milk until combined.

- Line a cupcake tin with patty cases and fill until ¾ full with mixture.

- Bake for 20 minutes.

- Leave the cupcakes in the tin for 5 minutes before transferring to a wire rack to cool.

- To prepare icing, blend together ricotta, honey, oil, coconut and orange juice in a food processor until smooth.

- Spoon icing over the cupcakes. Slice strawberries into quarters and place one quarter on top of each cupcake.

chocolate-coated strawberries

120g 70% dark chocolate

16 to 20 strawberries

- Melt dark chocolate.

- Cut the base off the strawberries so they sit flat. Dip each stawberry halfway in the chocolate, tip first.

- Cover a tray with silver foil and place the chocolate-coated strawberries on the tray to set.

- Refrigerate for at least 30 minutes until set.

Index